REA

ACPL ITEM
DISCARD

3 1833 04431 5817

S0-AUF-011

TIME TO NEGOTIATE

Guidelines for Pastors to Follow
When Salary Support Is Considered

Hilbert J. Berger

FRIENDSHIP PRESS • NEW YORK

ACKNOWLEDGMENTS

The following credits express our appreciation to the publishers and writers who have allowed us to use their materials in this book.

Cover and cartoons, From *Mirror For Chief Oikonomos* by Jack V. Reeve and Hilbert J. Berger. Reprinted with permission from the Commission on Stewardship, National Council of the Churches of Christ in the U.S.A. Copyright © 1967. Illustrations by Dave Rusch.

Page 33, From a "Checklist" by Lyle Schaller. Reprinted by permission of Lyle Schaller.

Copyright © 1973 by Friendship Press, Inc.
Printed in the United States of America

To Geneva
my wife
who like many other
wives has known
economic injustice because
minister-husbands
have refused to become
involved in the process
by which pastoral support
is determined.

contents

foreword

The brief is seldom prepared when ministers stand to plead their case for salary support. Their counsel, in most cases, is solely themselves. They stand in the vanguard of the do-it-yourselfers!

Hilbert J. Berger, with 24 years' experience in the art of local pastor, as it relates to salary negotiations, has provided a much-needed handbook.

Time to Negotiate is a clarion call for pastors to probe their understanding of ministry, clarify misty areas, ventilate musty cubicles where thwarted dreams have been stored, evaluate accurately family needs and to stand, ready and prepared, to present their cause and request commensurate financial reward.

Mr. Berger has provided a philosophy of contemporary negotiating procedures. He has, however, moved beyond the academic. Serving the local pastor as correspondent counselor he provides step-by-step directives for building the case and pleading it before the proper local church committee, thus providing the opportunity for a more just decision.

For those thousands of do-it-yourselfers who feel they must stand mute when the verdict of next year's salary is read, *Time to Negotiate* should be most welcome. For some who have accepted poverty as a ministerial virtue and others who feed a persecution complex on salary committee decision, the document will seem heresy. It is my belief that Mr. Berger has provided timely and contemporary assistance for pastors and local church salary committees.

Nordan C. Murphy
Director of Stewardship
National Council of the Churches
of Christ in the U.S.A.

introduction

This book is written to provide a bit of adrenalin to the harassed and beleaguered pastors at the time of their greatest tension.

At least once each year some group of lay persons caucuses to formulate a recommendation for pastoral support. Every fall for many years I agonized through those anxious hours. It wasn't until I became involved in the whole process that reasonable support was recommended.

I have a letter in my files in which a lay person writes, "the pastor's salary is a concern of the laymen and the pastor should not be involved in the process to determine it. It is the one authority left to laymen."

This book is written for those who disagree with that statement. It is written for those pastors who seek to give dignity and meaning to their office and who are convinced that "a worker deserves his wages" (Luke 10:7b).

The kind of participatory experience described in this book calls for careful preparation by the pastors. They must be willing to encourage a full and impartial investigation of their ministry and stewardship.

Lay persons may see in this procedure a way in which they can be helpfully related to their pastor, by making the determination of pastoral support a meaningful experience based upon careful negotiations, rather than a careless action based upon the pastor's popularity.

It is my hope that these simple guidelines will help to bring adequate support to every pastor who deserves it.

In every local church there is a committee which deals

with matters relating to the pastor's relationship to that local church. This committee often serves in a consultant relationship to him/her and once each year is asked to recommend the items related to pastoral support. In this book, this committee is referred to as the pastor-parish relations committee.

I am indebted to Mr. Jack Frye, a staff man with Profession's Economic Counsel of Chicago, who has checked out this material to see if it remains true to good negotiating practices and has entered into many helpful discussions with me during its preparation.

Hilbert J. Berger
1973

3 1833 04431 5817

1

the negotiating style

One afternoon as I was flying out of Washington, D.C., I learned that the man sitting beside me had just served as the chief labor negotiator of a contract for the nurses in a nearby city. After we became acquainted I said to him, "I know many pastors who need your help!" He quickly responded, "Why don't pastors organize?" I reminded him that in certain areas in America, Roman Catholic pastors had organized. But this did not satisfy him, since the organizing of the Roman Catholic clergy was an effort on behalf of the clergy to be heard by the Roman Catholic hierarchy. He felt that pastors should organize to secure better salary contracts. He went on to say that we live in a world where employers *expect* employees to organize and to negotiate. I was not especially interested when he said that pastors should organize (I feel this might only further fracture and separate clergy and lay relationships), but when he mentioned that we live in a society where employers *expect* employees to negotiate, I listened to him more carefully. It is, indeed, time to negotiate.

Ministers are in an isolated and very difficult and vulnerable position. A pastor is subject to collective bargaining in reverse! There is an "organized" collective employer (the church) dealing with an individual employee. The church has a representative body (a pastor-parish relations committee) who represents its membership as the employer, but the pastor, in many cases the *only* employee, has no one to bargain on his behalf. He/she, in fact, stands over against the entire membership in the matter of pastoral support considerations. Unfortunately, we have not trained our pastors to stand at this point of critical need.

There is available considerable printed and audiovisual material to give counsel and guidance to the lay members of a pastor-parish relations committee. One denomination, for instance, has produced a work kit for this purpose. The kit includes a cassette tape and guidebooks that relate to the work of a pastor-parish relations committee. No one will question the importance of the members of a pastor-parish relations committee knowing their responsibility and of their being trained to perform that responsibility. I am concerned, however, because most pastors have not learned to relate to a pastor-parish relations committee in economic matters and therefore all sorts of traumatic moments precede the decision to recommend the pastoral support for the next year.

Pastors have not learned to relate to pastor-parish relations committees in economic matters.

The labor negotiator informed me that the first thing he does in negotiating a contract is to make sure that those persons he represents have a clear understanding of their worth as workers. Similarly, before a pastor attempts to enter into negotiations with his pastor-parish relations committee, there are questions that he must ask himself. What is the most important work of a minister? Is it to preach? To visit? To counsel? To make firm pronouncements on moral issues? To teach? To offer the sacraments? To be a witness to Christ? To be a husband and a father? He must attempt to discover what gift it is that he has to share, and he must clearly have resolved his mission for Christ in that parish.

Not until a pastor has established a certainty of his ministry and is no longer content to allow the lay members of the pastor-parish relations committee to make decisions without the benefit of important data that he should be presenting to them is he in a position to begin planning to negotiate his salary.

Here are six guidelines to assist ministers in preparing for meaningful negotiations:

1. The pastor should be thoroughly familiar with data related to consumer prices and living standards in the community, average incomes, general conditions of economics in the community and the ability of the church to pay. He must gather this data and be prepared to make it available to his pastor-parish relations committee in writing. He may be able to get some of this data from the finance committee, or he may wish to enlist a small committee from his pastor-parish relations committee to help him obtain this information which will be included in the document he will prepare for the committee.

2. The pastor should be prepared to discuss pastoral support as now being received by other pastors in the community, and should, by comparison, know the salary and fringe benefits of such persons as the local high school principal as a reference for comparison. He should also be fully aware of the salary guidelines which may or may not have been set down by his denomination. He must remember that these guidelines are always minimum guidelines and are never to be considered other than minimum guidelines. The pastor must put the minimum salaries data into the document he is preparing for presentation to the pastor-parish relations committee.

3. The pastor must be willing to be candid and open in his negotiations with the pastor-parish relations committee. He must seek assurance from the committee that what he says and the documents he presents will be held in the strictest confidence. He should be ready to discuss the particular work load which he sees this congregation placing upon its pastor. He should be ready to express clearly the opportunities he sees for an effective ministry in this particular congregation. He should be ready to enunciate ways in which he feels he can have his particular ministry at this appointment. He should be ready to express what he feels is happening to him as he continues to serve in this congregation.

4. The pastor should be ready to present accurate data related to inflation and the cost of living. He must also be ready to talk freely about the tax situation as it affects him. Here is a point at which many people need to know the facts. There are many families who believe that pastors do not pay taxes, and that pastors get discounts on everything they purchase. The pastor must also clarify his position regarding honorariums or gratuities. Many families think that pastors receive a considerable amount of money for special services that they perform such as speeches, weddings, baptisms, funerals, etc. Many pas-

tors do not accept honorariums or gratuities of any kind, at least from their membership, and if this is so, this fact should be made known to the pastor-parish relations committee. It would be most appropriate for the pastor to be ready to inform the committee of the exact amount of cash he received in the past twelve months aside from his salary.

5. The pastor must be ready to present data related to total pastoral support. The area of fringe benefits is often over dramatized by lay persons, and minimized by pastors. It is important that the facts be in the hands of those who seek to negotiate. These facts can best be gathered by the pastor. (One fact that should not be overlooked is the 1971 report by Bankers Life indicating that the average contract negotiated in 1971 had fringe benefits averaging 26 percent of the total package.) The pastor must be prepared to itemize the cost of his travel related to the fulfilling of his assignment as pastor. He must clearly indicate his desire for continuing education on a regular basis, and the importance of this today for an effective ministry. He must also be clear about the goals to be achieved through continuing education. He must clearly indicate his feelings concerning the quality and the value of the housing that is provided for his family. He must be prepared to talk about other pastoral support problems such as insurance, both health and life insurance, about utility expenses and vacation benefits. He must help the committee to understand that when they set the figure of the cash salary they have dealt only with a part of their responsibility to recommend pastoral support. (See page 55 for a list of resources to help the pastor gather this data.)

Pastors must have a clear understanding of their worth as workers.

6. Most importantly, the pastor must be able to define what might be called economic respectability—not as money but as a status which will allow him indepen-

dence, dignity and an opportunity for a freedom to "minister." The pastor may wish to submit to this negotiating table evidence of his good money management procedures and an indication of the family life goals that have been determined by his family. If he has special economic responsibilities, or special needs that are approaching, he should be ready and willing to make these known to the pastor-parish relations committee.

When the pastor has done all of the homework required for adequate preparation of these six items he is then ready to take certain necessary steps that must precede all negotiations.

The guidelines for preparation might look something like this:

- The pastor should meet with the chairperson of the pastor-parish relations committee and arrange in advance for the pastoral support item to be on the agenda of the committee for its annual review. He must make it clear to the chairperson and to all members of the committee that this meeting is the beginning of a process which will determine pastoral support recommendations. The announcement of the meeting to the committee members should indicate that the pastor is preparing a document for presentation to the committee to help them in establishing the pastoral support recommendations for the coming year.

- The pastor may wish to discuss this matter of pastoral support with his district, synod, presbytery, state, conference or judicatory executive.

- The pastor must make certain that the meeting time for the pastor-parish relations committee—to discuss pastoral support—is at a time when members of the committee can give their undivided attention to this matter in an unhurried way. This meeting should not be held in

the pastor's home, nor should it be held in the home of a member of the committee. It should be held in a place where all members of the committee and the pastor may feel completely comfortable in expressing all of their mutual concerns.

2

the organization of the negotiating process

The First Meeting

The goal: *To hear the pastor's proposals, to answer questions and consider data. No final decisions are to be made at this meeting.*

The first meeting of the pastor-parish relations committee, concerning the building of a recommendation for pastoral support, should have as its major agenda item the report of the pastor. Negotiators indicate that the whole process in negotiation is *initiated* on the employee's side. It is only after a meeting or two that the employer responds to proposals. As I stated before, the first obligation of a negotiator is to make sure that those persons he/she represents clearly understand their worth as workers. Therefore it is only fitting that the pastor's proposal to the pastor-parish relations committee be prefaced with a very clear-cut resumé which plainly indicates his preparation for the task which is present in that parish. It should include a comprehensive statement on the meaning of the Christian ministry as he now sees it. A pastor will submit with this proposal written justification for each financial proposal that he presents. A clear exposure of needs is a necessity. He must be willing to express what peculiar financial responsibilities are his, such as educational debts, extensive medical expenses, etc. This is the point at which he *may* wish to submit his family money management and spending plan. Here is where he will indicate the goals which his family has established that are affected by salary support recommendations which this committee will make. The pastor must be prepared to accept and even encourage all members of the committee to question the proposals which he has made.

The attitude and the style for the negotiations will be established largely by the attitude and style of the pastor. As the pastor presents his resumé and statement concerning his understanding of the ministry, and as he presents his proposals, he must use great care to avoid any attitude that would indicate that he is serving an ultimatum. At no point should he suggest through his attitude that he is threatening the committee. Threats only give the other side an excuse to break off negotiations. The pastor must be careful not to establish deadlines. Justification and explanation for each item should avoid any hint of defensiveness—defensive attitudes negate communications and progress in negotiations. The negotiations should start early enough in the fall to allow investigation of each proposal and of the ministry being considered for funding in the new year.

A pastor should take care that he does not present lengthy or detailed figures in this initial proposal and that he does not offer all of his arguments for the proposals. It will be important to save certain data and documentation for the anticipated rebuttal. Too much data can look like a "snow job" and baffle the committee.

A detailed outline for the document which the pastor is to present at this first meeting will be given in a later section (see p. 26).

It may be necessary for the pastor to submit additional facts, in writing, on points that are questioned during the meeting. (It seems quite unlikely that an issue as real and important as pastoral support should be settled in one short meeting.) Proposals for significant amounts of change may be shocking. It is usually in the interest of the negotiator to keep the discussion going and to avoid getting final answers at this first meeting. A proposal for a certain benefit or plan that cannot be implemented immediately might become an established goal for the future.

After the committee has received the report and the proposals from the pastor, these items should be duplicated in sufficient quantities so that each member of the committee can have a copy. The pastor-parish relations committee should have ample time to review these proposals and to discuss them. It is extremely important that the committee be reminded that these proposals are not for general distribution or even for general discussion; they are presented to the pastor-parish relations committee as a resource to enable it to fulfill its obligation to recommend adequate pastoral support.

At this first meeting it is also important that all questions are answered and a further meeting date established. Care must be given that no quick decisions are arrived at, and there must be an awareness that time may take care of some of the shock which new proposals may bring to members of the committee.

Face-to-face discussion is the basis for meaningful negotiations.

There must be time for any clarification the committee desires. The honesty required for this kind of clarification will set the tone for negotiation of crises that may come later. The pastor-parish relations committee is not only determining total support, it is practicing, in a very pragmatic way, a style of operation. This should be a major factor in persuading the pastor to take the steps outlined in this handbook. It is his security for the future, and the congregation's!

There will be a general reaction among members of the committee that "there is more to this job than I thought." Yet there will develop a sense of pride in the significance of the role they play and the building of the tradition of the pastor-parish relations committee as a highly important committee. This may help to strengthen the work of the committee during the remainder of the year.

The Second Meeting

The goal: *To provide time for the pastor-parish relations committee to carefully consider the document presented by the pastor.*

20

The second meeting in this series, designed to negotiate pastoral support, is a meeting for the pastor-parish relations committee. The pastor does not have to be present at this particular meeting, but should be aware of the fact that it is scheduled and is being held. This meeting should be scheduled within a few days following the first meeting when the pastor has made his proposals.

During the days between the first and the second meetings the members of the pastor-parish relations committee will have in hand copies of the document which was prepared by the pastor.

The committee needs to be reminded again that this document is *not* for general discussion or general distribution, but that it is a working document for the pastor-parish relations committee, designed to help it fulfill its obligation to recommend pastoral support.

At this meeting the chairperson of the pastor-parish relations committee must emphasize the group's role as the primary functioning committee to aid the pastor in making his ministry effective. They do this by being available for counsel and keeping him advised concerning conditions within the congregation as they affect relations between the pastor and the people. This, of course, is the year-round responsibility of the committee. At this particular meeting the committee needs to discuss the role of the minister as they see it. This might be done by asking such questions as: Do we expect our pastor to provide helpful and inspiring worship services? Do we expect him to preach an excellent sermon every Sunday? Do we expect him to visit the sick and shut-ins? Do we expect him to set apart regular hours for counseling persons in need? Do we expect him to do all the office work and run the mimeograph? Do we expect him to call in all of the homes of our members? Do we expect him to direct the youth program and teach in the church school? Do we expect him to represent the voice of the church in the affairs of our city? Do we expect him to give direction to our stewardship program? Do we expect him to be the general business manager of the church? Do we really expect him to work all of the time?

What would be reasonable expectations in this parish as we think of the role of our pastor?

What are our assumptions as to the role of our pastor?

No matter how well equipped the committee may be, it might be difficult to deal with these questions without the pastor being present. What work is done must be considered tentative and subject to negotiation with the pastor.

After the committee has worked through these questions, it should then take another look at the pastor's statement concerning his understanding of the Christian ministry. As the committee discusses this document, notations should be made along the margin so that as negotiations continue, the most important questions can be lifted up when the pastor is present. It must be noted that decisions will be made only when the pastor is present. Face-to-face discussions for decisions is the basis for meaningful negotiations.

After the committee has refreshed its mind about its own existence, after it has worked through its expectations in regard to its pastor, and after it has looked once more at the pastor's statements concerning the ministry, it can then proceed to consider the proposals that appear on the pages following the pastor's statements (see page 49).

It is important that the committee begin with the proposals listed in Section A first. After this section has been reviewed and discussed, the committee then moves to Section B, then to Section C and finally to Section D (see pages 29–33, 49–52).

The committee may wish to present a document to the pastor for the next meeting or it may wish to present certain counter proposals. Whatever its decision, it should be remembered that this process is designed as a full participatory process. *Negotiating is not simply reaching a compromise between two positions, but is a search for accommodations that goes behind the stated demands and figures to the real needs.*

The chairperson and secretary of the committee shall be responsible for any written report of this meeting that is to be a part of the next meeting with the pastor.

The Third Meeting

The goal: *To begin the actual process of negotiating.*

It would seem appropriate for the person chairing the pastor-parish relations committee to briefly summarize the reactions of the committee as related to the pastor's statement concerning the meaning of the ministry. Members of the committee should indicate the parts of the statement with which they strongly agree, and should enter into a dialogue with the pastor concerning the areas of his report where there may be some slight difference of opinion. Until the matter of the rationale for the ministry in this particular parish is settled, it will be impossible to have an intelligent discussion concerning total pastoral support. Thus, this third meeting may be devoted entirely to the matter of establishing the style, direction, goals and emphases for the ministry in this parish. This will have been done already if the committee has been meeting regularly. They will need to look at it again, however, at this time.

Negotiation leaves no place for feather-bedding.

The first year of a pastorate demands general statements, and, as events call for clarification of positions, succeeding years would call for more and more specific proposals. In a sense this is an annual review of the year's work and a summary look ahead. Care should be taken not to negotiate permanent commitments.

The further agenda for this committee will consist of an item-by-item consideration of the pastor's proposals. This item-by-item consideration may necessitate another meeting. (The total outline for this meeting will be more clearly understood when the pastor works through Chapter 3 which gives in detail the outline and the content for the development of the pastor's document.)

As the committee begins to consider his report item by

item, especially Sections A, B, C and D, the pastor should expect and, if necessary, formally request a definite answer to each item of his proposal. A record should be kept of the response which the committee makes to each of these proposals. Since the pastor would not make proposals that do not carry his moral conviction, he must be prepared to stick with these proposals until he has made all reasonable effort to validate them before the committee in relation to his ministry and mission and in the best interests of the church.

An additional factor, however, is that pastors, for the most part, have been either very dogmatic or extremely passive when it came to seeking adequate pastoral support. It may be true that few pastors know how to compromise, but negotiating *requires* compromise. It presumes that there are two sides to every question and both sides must be heard before just decisions can be made.

Negotiating requires compromise.

Many committees have denied certain pastoral support benefits to an experienced and effective minister causing him to seek another parish. Then, this same committee has *negotiated* with a new minister for the same benefits requested by the former minister, thus incurring unnecessary expenses and creating an emotional upheaval in the parish.

Make no mistake about it, it is time to negotiate. It is time for the pastor and the committee to discuss openly the question of total pastoral support. One person or committee can no longer be expected to represent both the employer (the local congregation) and the employee (the clergy). If honest negotiations are attempted, the role of the ineffectual loafer will surface very quickly. Negotiation leaves no place for featherbedding. Through this kind of open and honest evaluation and projection can come improved relationships, an understanding and assertion of the value and worth of the clergyman and the work he does, and the importance of this position of leadership for the health of the church. The pastor must be ready and willing to have his ministry totally exposed and evaluated.

The church expects the pastor-parish relations committee to have the concerns of the pastor as well as the concerns of the parish in mind as it recommends pastoral support. This is clearly reflected in the fact that most churches, through an administrative board, accept the recommendations of the pastor-parish relations committee. Pastors must learn the skills necessary for meaningful negotiating, so that adequate pastoral support can assure them of economic respectability and the freedom to have their ministry. To downgrade the importance of this desire for adequate support is to minimize the importance of the pastor's skills and ministry.

If differences are serious, the use of another person as intermediary or mediator might be considered. Sometimes such a person can assist in finding an area of accommodation while helping to avoid heated expressions of disagreement. It should be emphasized, however, that expressions of conflicting views, even heated exchanges, *are not necessarily harmful*. They may clear the air and improve relationships. If there is injustice, the pastor must not be afraid to confront it! This should not be considered as a confrontation experience as much as an opportunity for lay-clergy dialogue.

3

the pastor's document and the strategy

The goal: *To outline the structure of the pastor's document and to give specific and detailed guidance for the strategy relating to its structure and presentation to the committee.*

The Document

It is important that consideration be given to the style, form and content of the document the pastor will present to the first meeting of the pastor-parish relations committee.

The pastor has the full responsibility for the preparation of this document in careful consultation with his wife, family, and, if desired, a trusted ministerial friend, or his denominational judicatory official. He also may wish to use selected members of the committee to help him with data gathering. This is not an issue to be treated lightly. He must carefully research the statistics, realizing that this document will form the basis for decisions that will govern his family's economic life for the new year, his style of ministry and provide a basis for review each year to come.

The pastor's document should be typed in an easy-to-read form with sufficient margins to allow notations or adjustments that may be made as discussions continue.

The document should include:

1. A resumé or informal autobiographical statement of the pastor's life and education.

   A. This may need to be given in detail if there is a new pastor-parish relations committee, or if he is a relatively new pastor in this situation.

B. This resumé or autobiographical statement may contain experiences that he believes have contributed toward making him act, react and think as he does at this time.

2. A clear and concise statement on the meaning of the ministry as he sees it.

   A. A statement of the development of his understanding of the ministry. He may take this opportunity to indicate ways in which his attitudes and opinions have changed or are in the process of being formulated. He may want to use a section to outline ways in which he feels his ministry can be a fulfilling experience in this particular parish.

   B. He may wish to lift up those conditions which he feels are inhibiting his ministry in this community.

   C. He may wish to discuss in this document his personal life goals as related to the ministry.

   D. He will want to make a statement as to how he believes his ministry can be shared with the laity of this parish and how the laity can strengthen his ministry during the next year, and how, through the support of his leadership, the laity can participate in their ministry. This is a very important aspect of pastoral support.

   E. He may wish to make a list of his assumptions concerning his ministry.

3. Statements concerning the ways which he believes the pastor-parish relations committee can specifically be of help to him as he seeks to fulfill his ministry during the next year. This will help the committee see its year-round responsibilities, many of which can be separated from the salary setting experience.

4. Data to be presented to the committee which will help it to determine the total pastoral support.

A. The A section of the document prepared for the pastor-parish relations committee will deal with matters that have nothing to do with finances or economics—the non-cost items such as rights, privileges, procedures, freedoms, responsibilities.

B. The B section of this document will deal with matters of rules or work arrangements that may have some cost but are not strictly economic cost items.

C. The C section of this document will deal with matters related to fringe benefits.

D. The D section of this document will deal with the cash salary item.

Beyond these facts, the pastor will want to anticipate the kind of questions and criticisms that are going to be made of each statement, and be prepared to have supportive material at hand to deal with it. This is what is known as anticipated rebuttal material. That is, after the pastor has made his main case, he then must be prepared to support his propositions extensively.

This procedure keeps the pastor from putting in the body of the document lengthy and detailed figures that might overwhelm or disinterest a committee. It is better to pick one figure, perhaps the average or the most significant, and in this way give more authority to the whole argument. References may be made in the document to supportive material such as a chart or a table of figures. This style often tends to reduce arguments that arise when large numbers of statistics are presented.

The Strategy

It will be clear immediately that this strategy is a *reverse strategy* from that which most pastors have employed when dealing with the matter of pastoral support. They have always started with the item of the cash salary and then wondered why it was difficult to get the committee to consider seriously some of the items related to fringe benefits or non-cost concerns. When the matter of the cash salary is settled first, the non-economic matters are frequently lost or, at least, do not receive careful consideration. Once the committee has concentrated on the cash questions it often wants to quit.

Those in the business of negotiating are adamant in resisting all attempts to make a package deal out of the negotiations. The negotiations must proceed item by item and whatever the total is, that becomes the total, rather than settling on a total as a package negotiation.

Let us look in more detail at these four areas of strategy as outlined.

Section A

Section A, the first items to be written into the document and the first matters to be settled, are those that may have nothing to do with finances or economics. These are called the non-cost items such as relationships, rights, privileges and procedures. It is here that the matter of a Pastor's Discretionary Fund should be discussed.

When cash salary is settled first, non-economic matters are frequently lost.

This section will vary according to the life-style of the pastor and the life-style of his church. In this particular section there must be a clarification as to the role of the pastor. It is in this section of the document that the pastor will try to identify clearly for his committee the role which he sees as a valid ministry in that particular parish. It is here that he will enunciate the kind of relationships he feels he must be free to establish and cultivate in order to fulfill his ministry. It is in this section that he will submit for examination his style of administration, his overall planning, his design for preaching, his relationship concerning vital issues, his sense of personal well-being, his concern for his family's well-being and so forth. It is here that the pastor will deal with the adequacy of the parsonage and its equipment. Everything, in other words, that supports the ministry to which the congregation has called him and frees him to

29

give unobstructed attention to this ministry is up for discussion.

Though a pastor-parish relations committee should be dealing with these concerns throughout the year, it may be appropriate for the committee to spend one full evening dealing with these non-cost items prior to the decisions that must determine the full pastoral support package.

Section B

Section B in the pastor's document to the pastor-parish relations committee contains the matter of rules or work arrangements that have some cost but are not strictly cost items.

This section, too, will vary greatly according to the size of the congregation and the work style of the pastor. It is in this section that such matters as office space, office equipment and secretarial staff must be considered and discussed. It is here that the pastor-parish relations committee may consider the kind of personnel help that may be needed to support their pastor in the ministry which he is projecting for that parish. It is during the discussion of this particular section that the pastor-parish relations committee may want to make certain that the pastor is going to maintain office hours or that he be absent from the office one day per week, or that he edit or not edit the parish paper, or that he emphasize some particular program or de-emphasize another or that he give his major concern to the youth. It is here that the car allowance should be considered. (Note it is not a fringe benefit.) When the car allowance is considered, it should be a realistic proposal, not a token proposal.

Section C

Section C will deal with matters commonly known as fringe benefits: housing allowance, pension, health and hospitalization insurance, accident insurance, life insurance, social security payments, perquisites and honorariums, support for the pastor's program for personal continuing education, library fund, entertainment fund and vacation time.

A 1971 report indicates that labor contracts negotiated in the first six months of 1971 contained fringe benefits equal to 26 percent of the contract. This percentage will continue to increase. One of the problems in the local churches is that fringe benefits have not been carefully considered item by item and therefore some pastors are able to enjoy a wide variety of benefits while others are accepting salary contracts devoid of itemized fringe benefits.

What are often called fringe benefits are frequently not benefits at all but really necessities for security and health. Many churches have thought that to pay a little more salary and not consider the fringe benefits was an equitable way of dealing with the matter of pastoral support. But the fact is that a little more salary does not make up for the fact that a man has less insurance benefits or less vacation. The pastor still wants and deserves a vacation. If this requires the expense of guest preachers, so be it.

Fringe benefits are often not benefits but real necessities.

A housing allowance may be considered a fringe benefit, but a church-owned parsonage should not be considered a fringe benefit. Any salary represented by the parsonage is lost to the future. The pastor is unable to build equity in his home and thus have a house to live in when he moves from his last parsonage. It must be remembered that if the pastor is to have a home, he must build into his budget an amount that would provide for a house quite apart from that which is called the parsonage. The care, upkeep, maintenance, repairs and improvements of the parsonage should in no way be considered pastoral support. This is a very sticky problem to most pastors and to many lay persons. Many lay persons find that the mortgage on their home and the upkeep and improvements require up to 25 percent of their income. As they see the pastor free from these worries they view the benefits of a parsonage beyond any evaluation the pastor would place on it. Make no mistake about it, when a parsonage is furnished the pastor requires less cash salary, *but how much less salary?* If the church is willing to provide a retirement home for the pastor, then I would suggest that the full rental potential should be considered additional salary. In most cases, churches do not provide retirement homes for pastors. Therefore, some provision must be made for income sufficient to allow the pastor to save at least an amount equal to the equity he would be building if he were purchasing a home, and in an inflationary economy this is a considerable amount.

Section D

Section D, the final section of the document to be presented to the pastor-parish relations committee, deals with the matter of the actual cash salary. The pastor should be prepared to document whatever proposition or proposal he makes at this particular point in his statement. *It may be difficult to keep the committee from considering this item first,* but it must be emphasized that to allow the committee to consider this item first is to be assured that the other three areas of concern will get less than the specific attention that they need.

Committees function better if they have *more than one* salary figure to look at. It may be that the pastor will want to present three such salary figures. He may want to present a figure listed as minimum (this may be considerably higher than his present salary). He may then wish to present a desirable salary figure and, finally, he may wish to present a figure based upon what he believes this church could pay as a cash salary if they considered more carefully their stewardship obligations, the work they want done and their pastor's needs.

In this particular section the pastor should present, with the document, certain facts related to the cost of living. These facts may be obtained from the U.S. Department of Labor, The Bureau of Labor Statistics, Washington, D.C. By applying the consumer price index to the figures which he receives from the Federal Government he has figures to support the salary proposals. He may wish to list what is happening generally to salaries and wages. He may want to note that the salaries of the city employees of New York City have increased 15 percent each year during the past five years, or in that particular period of five years there has been a 75 percent increase. This is about the same increase in salaries given to Federal Government employees over the past five years. How do these figures compare with the increases granted to the pastor of this local church? What is the minimum salary set by your denomination for those who are just beginning their ministry?

Lyle Schaller, of Yokefellow Institute, Richmond, Indiana, has put together a checklist that the committee should consider.

"Checklist"

1. How does the compensation (base salary, travel allowance, payment of utilities in the parsonage and hospitalization insurance) compare with what other comparable congregations are doing in this district and this conference?

2. How does the total compensation compare with that paid by other comparable Lutheran, Presbyterian, Baptist, United Methodist, Episcopal, and United Church of Christ congregations in this community?

3. How does the compensation compare with that paid to the local superintendent of schools? (High school principal?)

4. How does the total compare with what this congregation paid in 1968? Has the increase been consistent with the increase in wages and salaries for teachers, social workers and others with similar training?

5. Does this congregation pay a car allowance? How does this amount compare with the actual expense incurred by the pastor in church related travel?

6. Is there money in the church budget to pay for part or all of the cost of continuing education programs for the minister?

7. Should the pastor receive a merit increase in recognition of the quality of his work?

8. Should the pastor's experience and tenure be taken into account in setting the salary figure?

9. If the congregation pays a housing allowance instead of providing a parsonage, what is the amount of the allowance? Has this been increased in recent years? Is the current amount a realistic figure?

10. If the pastor moves in the near future, is the amount now being paid sufficient to secure a new minister with the same training and experience? You may need to check with your denominational offices.

11. What is the minimum salary set for ministers graduating from seminary in June? How does that compare with the salary paid by this congregation? (Remembering that this is minimum!)

12. Does the age of the minister's children and their year in school say anything to the salary question in this congregation?

13. How will this decision be interpreted?

People still believe that pastors do not pay taxes.

The amount of the salary increase granted the pastor usually is interpreted in various ways. An increase of five percent, for example, represents a salary reduction in terms of buying power. Is this how this recommendation is intended to be interpreted? An increase of two or three percent represents a substantial reduction, and could be interpreted as an invitation to the pastor to move. Is this the intended recommendation? An increase of fifteen percent could be interpreted as recognition of exceptional service, *or* it could be interpreted as an effort to make up for previous pattern. Which is intended? Sometimes the reasons are more significant than the amount of the increase. It often is helpful for all concerned if the reasons are clearly stated for the recommendation on the pastor's salary.

As a pastor seeks to support his cash salary proposal or proposals it seems appropriate that he should give some indication of his family's stewardship. It may be that he will wish to present in some detail the peculiar financial obligations which he and his family have for the coming year. Since it has been pre-determined that this would need to be an open style of negotiation, the pastor should be willing to submit in some detail his responsibilities and his family's financial goals for the future. There are many persons in our churches who still believe that pastors do not pay taxes and that they receive large honorariums and perquisites, that they receive 10 percent discounts at all stores and that they receive many cash gifts, personal gifts and generous amounts of food donated to them by the families of the church. It may be that in some situations some of these facts yet apply, but for the most part, pastors carry a heavy burden of taxes which includes full payment of social security tax and income taxes. Most pastors do not receive large amounts of money or special discounts or additional gifts. If the pastor is willing to deal honestly at this point he can be of great help in setting a workable style for negotiating the cash salary. He can do this by carefully listing those discounts, special gifts, honorariums and perquisites that he received during the last year. It is quite likely that when these are totalled they will not be a significant influence in the negotiation of a base salary.

Finally, data for supporting the cash proposal should contain facts related to the comparison of salaries that pastors are receiving in nearby churches and in other same level occupations.

1. List cash salaries and total packages now being paid in other congregations nearby. Journals will provide a source of information, but remember, these statistics are always more than one year out-of-date. Obtain up-to-date statistics.

2. List compensation being paid or being considered in other denominations.

3. List average incomes for the area.

4. List compensation to other professions in the community, such as superintendent of schools, public school teachers with master's degrees and equal years of service.

5. List recent news articles which relate content of local labor contracts.

6. Do not list all your data. Save some for the conversations and negotiations.

As the pastor begins to prepare his document from these guidelines, he should realize that not all of the items presented in this proposal will be accepted. They will not all be accepted even if he has done his homework and, by way of this document, has given some vision to the pastor-parish relations committee. By means of this document he will be able to introduce ideas that are fresh and in some instances revolutionary. Even though all of these items are not likely to be accepted the first time they are presented, if they appear in his report this year they will not sound so revolutionary when they appear next year.

As I mentioned before, there will certainly be some serious differences; and some honest confrontations may develop through this kind of negotiating experience. These confrontations should not be ignored, and some resolution of these conflicts should be sought. It may be that the pastor will need to get assistance. At least he will need to seek some positive management of these conflicts if they cannot be resolved.

There are three kinds of assistance that he may seek: the assistance of a *conciliator,* a *mediator* or an *arbitrator.*

A *conciliator* is a person with no official capacity; he is a person who helps both sides to continue a discussion until *they* have found an answer. A conciliator is, in some sense of the word, a facilitator. He keeps the discussion going so that the parties themselves work out an agreement.

A *mediator* is a person who joins in the act or process of negotiating and lifts up for the conflicting parties those discussions or proposals that can promote reconciliation, settlement or compromise. Though he has no authority in the dispute, he enters into the dispute in a very real way to help bring about a settlement.

An *arbitrator* is a neutral in the dispute. The issues of the dispute are referred to him and *he decides* for both sides. In certain cases this is accepted as binding arbitration. This means that whatever decision the arbitrator makes becomes binding on both sides of the negotiating experience. It would be a rare exception if an arbitrator is used, but it is an option open in the negotiating process.

It is quite possible that a district, synod, presbytery or state denominational executive could effectively serve as a conciliator, a mediator or an arbitrator. There may be other ways a judicatory executive could help in the negotiating process.

As the pastor puts his document together and produces enough copies of it for the pastor-parish relations committee, it is important that he *not* run mathematical totals on any of the sections of this report. This means also that he will not run a total on all of the proposals. Every effort must be made to *resist the presentation of a package proposal* to the committee. Let the committee consider item by item and then let the total be whatever it will be.

Chapter 5 is a sample document that has been prepared illustrating the procedures and the forms which have been discussed so far in this chapter. The pastor will want to review carefully this document and then build from it the instrument which is most appropriate for presentation to his pastor-parish relations committee.

4

alternatives for a
multi-staff church

The goal: *To explore a style for negotiating pastoral support which could be appropriate to staff situations where the pastor-parish relations committee must establish support for more than one ordained person, as well as other professional staff persons.*

The guidelines in this book are prepared for pastors who wish to enter into the determining of pastoral support, but there are many churches with more than one ordained employee. Who speaks for those ordained persons who are not the senior pastor? Who speaks for the non-ordained professional staff?

In most churches, there is a line of command which places the senior pastor in a position that allows him free dialogue with the pastor-parish relations committee. The other ordained members of the staff and the other professionals on the staff do not enjoy this free dialogue. They are often shut off from pastor-parish relations committee meetings and must rely on the senior pastor as being willing to carry their concerns and requests. In this uncomfortable position there can be few opportunities for meaningful negotiations. The situation is further complicated in that the senior pastor generally enjoys adequate support, while associates and assistants may struggle for economic survival. In a recent survey, I discovered that there is often a 50 percent differential between salary paid to senior pastors and salaries paid to assistants and associates. When an assistant's or an associate's salary is at a survival level and the senior pastor's salary is at the achievement level, we should begin to understand why there is often little cooperation and no creativity among assistants and associates and other professionals on the staff.

In many churches, the associate pastor or the assistant pastor is a career person. By that, I mean that these persons are not just out of a seminary, nor are they at the end of their ministry. They are capable, dedicated persons who do not desire the role of senior pastor. These persons must receive careful consideration when a design for negotiating pastoral support is adopted. If this is done, the support differential will not be so great between senior pastors and career assistants or associates.

The work of a pastor-parish relations committee in a multi-staff situation is not easy. If the committee enters into a meaningful dialogue with each ordained member of the staff, and builds support for his or her ministry, and if they carefully consider the role of all professional staff persons, being on the committee will be a time consuming but rewarding experience. Our concern here, however, is on the clergy side of negotiating. How can all ordained staff and other professional staff persons gain access to the counsel and support of the pastor-parish relations committee?

Who speaks for ordained persons who are not senior pastors?

Using the material of this book as the base style, several alternatives may be considered.

1. If the pastor-parish relations committee is willing and available, the total procedure of this book could be repeated for each ordained staff person and for each professional staff person. Under this plan, each person would prepare a document for review by the committee. This document would contain his or her autobiographical sketch, statement on the ministry, task, list of assumptions and the specific proposals for negotiating. In this alternative it would seem inappropriate for any proposal to be submitted to the pastor-parish relations committee without consultation with the senior pastor. His support will be necessary if any proposal is to receive full consideration.

In essence this alternative suggests that each staff person shall carry full responsibility for getting his needs before the pastor-parish relations committee and shall be his own chief negotiator with that committee!

2. Another alternative style for negotiating pastoral support in a multi-staff church might develop in the regular staff meeting. Here the total ministry of the church could be discussed, with each staff person free to express the needs and anxieties of his or her share of that ministry. In the staff meetings the needs of each member of the staff could be expressed and considered. In this dialogue helpful criticisms could be offered and a supportive style adopted.

It is possible that joint proposals could be made to the committee relating to housing, insurance, travel allowances, continuing education, sabbatical leaves and the overall ministry which the staff sees itself sharing. Joint proposals would carry additional influence in negotiations and would lessen the possibility of inequities between senior staff members and assistants and associates. Joint proposals could carry the best thinking of all of the members of the staff and would give evidence of a team ministry. When joint proposals are being negotiated it will be imperative that all members of the professional staff be present at the pastor-parish relations committee meeting with full privilege of entering into the discussions.

This alternative style for negotiating pastoral support in a multi-staff church would require the individual preparation of the autobiography, statement of ministry and a list of non-cost items and fringe benefits not listed in the joint proposal, as well as a cash salary proposal.

It is important to remember that in a negotiating style, no one, no group, presents a package for negotiating. Each item must be considered individually. It is important to remember and observe the order in which the committee is to consider each individual item—the cash salary proposal must be the last item considered.

3. Alternative number three for negotiating in a multi-staff church suggests that the senior pastor receive all of the proposals from all of the professional staff of the church. The senior pastor would then take all of these proposals to the pastor-parish relations committee for consideration and would sit as the chief negotiator for each and all members of the staff.

The proposals of the senior pastor may or may not be negotiated at the same time that the pastor-parish relations committee considers the proposals of the other members of the professional staff.

This alternative differs from the second alternative in that there are no joint proposals, and only the senior pastor is at the negotiating table with the pastor-parish relations committee.

This alternative style would suggest a complete openness among the staff so that conflicting and contradictory proposals would not be made. An agenda item at regular staff meeting could begin to deal with mutual concerns and needs many weeks before final proposals were submitted to the senior pastor for presentation to the committee.

General guidelines in this book for the presentation and preparation of the pastor's document should be followed by all professional staff persons.

This alternative requires full and complete confidence in the negotiating ability of the senior pastor.

This alternative should not be forced on the staff but could be a style they would elect.

4. Alternative number four for negotiating pastoral support in a multi-staff church suggests that the professional staff prepare individual pastoral documents according to the guidelines in this book.

The committee might consider the proposals of the

senior pastor while he sits as his own negotiator. Due process, according to the guidelines of this book, would require the investment of several weeks of the committee's time. During these negotiations with the senior pastor, certain guidelines and precedences could be established on behalf of the other professional staff persons. Proposals related to working style, office equipment, supporting staff, fringe benefits and even guidelines for salaries could be established.

After all of the senior pastor's proposals have been considered, other professional staff persons could come as individuals or as a group to have their proposals considered. The chief points of negotiating then would be at points where a precedent had not been established during the senior pastor's negotiations, or at these very points where exceptions need to be made.

Who speaks for the non-ordained professional staff?

5. Some churches have established salary schedules which call for a classification of all ordained clergy on the basis of education, experience, age, etc. In these churches negotiations can still be a factor in determining pastoral support, since established schedules usually deal only with the cash salary item. Today's professional employees must carefully consider the non-cost and fringe benefit items that often determine whether a cash salary is significant.

In a rapidly accelerated inflationary economy it may be necessary that the entire salary schedule be re-negotiated. This matter must be entered into by all ordained staff persons using a full and open negotiating approach to the salary schedule. This may mean that as a professional person he will need to get out of his neat little "box" which displays him as a person interested only in spiritual things.

It is my experience that lay people are much more willing to negotiate this matter of pastoral support than the clergy and other professional staff persons are willing to be involved in the process.

The pastor-parish relations committee must see its professional staff as key to the full ministry of the church, and they must be ready to make their work supportive. What I have offered here as alternative styles for negotiating pastoral support in a multi-staff church are all predicated on the assumption that the pastor-parish relations committee meets regularly during the year and consults frequently with all members of the staff in such matters as job analysis and personal problems. Unless meaningful dialogue has been established and continued throughout the year, it will be an unnatural and difficult experience to develop meaningful negotiations for pastoral support. Nevertheless, it must be done! It must be remembered that pastoral support is to be negotiated on an annual basis. This requires and allows flexibility in negotiating. This also requires the proposal of items that may not get serious consideration this year, but which will not be considered innovative when they have been a part of several annual proposals.

5

the pastor's document

This sample Pastor's Document should serve only as a guideline, not as an outline. Each pastor should use his or her own creativity in developing this statement.

I. Autobiographical Statement of I. Willbee Frank

I was born April 9, 1931, the third son of an Arkansas farmer. I had one sister. My parents were hard working people who early in life devoted themselves to the task of educating their children. Three of their four children graduated from college. All of them are self-employed.

My parents are lifelong members of Old First Church, Newburg, and both have served as members with leadership responsibility throughout the years. They are both living and still reside on their farm, but one of my brothers, having purchased a neighboring farm, also farms my parents' acreage.

I attended a rural grade school, a consolidated high school and graduated from our own church college in Arkadelphia. My seminary work was done at St. Paul School of Theology, Kansas City. I graduated there in 1955. I am married to the former Justa Beauty. We have three children, two sons and a daughter, who are all in high school. My wife is a graduate of the Westminster School of Music and is a member of the Organist Guild. She has had four years' experience as a high-school teacher, though she is not teaching at this time.

The major hobby of my family is travel. We have explored most areas of the United States with the help of our travel trailer. In 1967 we spent two months camping in Europe as we gave leadership to a European Family Camping Tour.

During the winter months our family increases by one person as Mrs. Frank's mother comes to live with us.

In the fall of next year our oldest son will begin his college work at Western State.

II. My View of My Ministry

I am certain that I was called of God to this specific ministry of a pastor, though I am convinced that all men are called of God to a ministry.

I have been educated for this special ministry at one of our church colleges and at one of our seminaries. I have been examined by conference committees and approved for ordination. I was ordained elder in 1957. I have had further study at Boston University in the area of pastoral counseling.

I have accumulated sixteen years of experience in this pastoral role. I served for three years as a pastor of a rural charge, eleven years as pastor of a suburban church, and this is the middle of my second year as pastor at this church.

I consider myself called of God, but not in the sense that this makes me odd, peculiar, special, particularly pious or unusual.

I am a person, created by God with certain potentials and distinctions that are particularly me. I am struggling, growing, adjusting, searching, sorting, deciding, specifying and becoming. All of this to the end that I may reach the full potential God has invested in me.

I see my job as that of a pastor—not as a manager, not as a director, not as one with status or authority, but as one of being in ministry with you. I see the role of pastor as one which is supporting, encouraging and enabling. I see the pastor as one who considers all persons as unique and his or her role as that of helping them to their full potential.

I consider myself a professional, not as one occupying a special niche in the social hierarchy, but as one specifically trained and committed to his task.

My motivation comes from the spirit, life and ministry of Jesus Christ, and an awareness of the tremendous evidence of need for reconciliation everywhere.

I am a citizen of this land and, therefore, I have political convictions. I do not intend to use the office of pastor to promote them, but I hold to the right to be involved in the political life of our community and nation.

I am specifically trained in stewardship and I anticipate opportunities to teach and train other pastors in this area of concern. This may, at times, require days of absence from my pastoral assignment. These requests and this time of absence will be put before this pastor-parish relations committee for its approval prior to any acceptance of these wider obligations.

I am interested in the district camping program, and expect to give several weeks to this work next summer.

I am not now active in ecumenical affairs.

I expect freedom in developing my ministry and I expect to give persons in this church freedom in developing their ministry.

III. I Have Certain Assumptions

I assume that:	*This may mean that:*
1. I will be expected to serve as chief administrator for this church.	1. I will need sufficient time in the office and sufficient staff to expedite this work.

1. We will need an additional secretary.
1. Some new office equipment will be necessary.

2. I will be expected to preach sermons that will maintain our present worship attendance and attract new families.

2. I will need sufficient time for research and study.
2. I will need additional funds for library needs.

3. This church will provide adequate housing for my family.

3. A program to renovate the parsonage will be necessary.
3. A new parsonage will be built or bought.
3. The old parsonage will be sold and I will receive a housing allowance.

4. I will be expected to have available a car for pastoral duties.

4. An adequate allowance will be made for travel expense.
4. The church will buy a car for me to use for these purposes.
4. A monthly report of mileage will be submitted for reimbursement to the church treasurer.

5. This church wishes to have its pastor well informed in the developing concerns of the ministry.

5. Annually the pastor will enroll in a school for a refresher course at the church's expense.
5. After 5 years of service the pastor will be given a 4-months' sabbatical for intensive study and recreation.

6. Pension, insurance and Social Security concerns for my family will be met.

6. This church will provide health and hospitalization insurance, a share of the cost of Social Se-

curity, enough term life insurance to protect the congregation against the crisis of the pastor's death.

7. This congregation does not want its pastor to seek additional salary from each wedding, funeral or baptism.

7. This church will carefully consider the establishment of an adequate cash salary for its pastor.

8. The matter of pastoral support is a mutual problem, and this committee will take seriously its responsibility to recommend adequate pastoral support to the administrative board.

8. We will spend the time necessary to explore all of the problems and privileges related to the office of pastor and to set in motion a plan for negotiating this matter using this document as a beginning point.

9. Pastoral support is too important to be settled in one quick meeting.

9. We will take the time to investigate this problem completely.

10. The salary paid by this church should be comparable to the salary paid in other churches of this size and in this area.

10. This will require some research on the part of members of this committee.

11. The salary and fringe benefits paid by this church should be comparable to that paid by other denominations in this area.

11. This will require research by this committee.

12. The negotiating style is a valid procedure.

12. We will face the matter of pastoral support through a full and open discussion.

(This list should be extended according to personal need.)

The Pastor's Report

Section A (Consider this Section first.)

The Need	The Proposal	Supporting Data	Committee Action
1. Help in the overall problems of church administration.	1. That personnel and equipment be considered that would relieve me of the total burden as chief administrator.	1. Up to 70 percent of my time is devoted to administration.	
2. A Pastor's study made more soundproof.	2. Insulation of the walls and the installation of a new door.	2. Counseling is very difficult when persons know that their voices can be heard by the church secretary or others in the church office.	
3. The kitchen at the parsonage is not adequate.	3. A consultant should be called in to design better use of and new equipment for the parsonage kitchen.	3. Cupboard space is inadequate. The standard here is far below the parish average.	
4. A three-bedroom home is not adequate for my family.	4. A recommendation should go to the Trustees for an additional bedroom and bathroom.	4. My wife's mother lives with us in the winter, increasing the problem.	
5. Regular meetings of this committee.	5. This committee should meet one time per month.	5. This would help avoid crisis decisions. Goals could be set according to church priorities.	
6. The establishment of a Pastor's Discretionary Fund.	6. The Finance Committee should be alerted to this need and suggest ways it may be funded.	6. Many opportunities to meet personal needs require that funds be available by the pastor to use at his discretion.	
7. An adequate vacation for the pastor and all staff.	7. Four weeks!	7. I have been employed by the same employer for 16 years.	

49

Section B (Consider this Section second.)

The Need	The Proposal Immediate	Goal	Supporting Data	Committee Action
1. Less than a seven-day work week.	1. Six-day work week.	1. Five-day work week.	1. The trend is to shorten working hours. Efficiency falls as hours extend.	
2. Adequate secretarial help to cover days off as well as hours out of the office.	2. One person full-time, one person one-half time.	2. Two full-time secretaries.	2. One secretary could serve as administrative secretary relieving me of some of the general administration.	
3. A full-time business manager.	3. Volunteer help.	3. Retiree.	3. As the church has grown, staff has not been enlarged.	
4. Adequate car allowance.	4. $1,000.	4. $1,500.	4. My federal income tax returns indicate a large expenditure of personal funds for this item.	
			4. Last year I was paid $700, but my tax allowance was $1,200.	

(Your list should be extended.)

Section C (Consider this Section third.)

The Need	The Proposal		Supporting Data	Committee Action
1. Utility allowance.	1. Gas	$200	1. These proposals are based upon last year's actual cost plus 4 percent.	
	1. Water	$36		
	1. Electricity	$180		
	1. Telephone	$120		

Item	Amount	Notes
2. Housing allowance in lieu of parsonage.	2. $3,600.	2. This would free the church from liabilities related to parsonage, furnishings, upkeep, repairs, improvements, insurance, etc.
		2. This would allow the pastor to build some equity and thus provide for retirement housing.
		2. This amount would be tax-exempt income.
3. Pension.	3. 12 percent of the pastor's cash salary.	3. This is not an elective.
4. Health and Hospitalization Insurance.	4. $300.	4. It is not an elective in our conference.
5. Accident Insurance.	5. $50.	5. Many churches are providing this coverage. This would provide $50,000 coverage.
6. Term Life Insurance.	6. $190 buys $20,000.	6. Recognizing the level of pension payments coming to the wife of a man of 15 years' experience, this would protect the church against crisis.
7. Social Security Payments.	7. $468.	7. Amount paid by other employers—declared income.
8. Support on Continuing Education.	8. $350.	8. Support for a two-week refresher course.

Section D (Consider this Section last.)

The Need	The Proposal	Supporting Data	Committee Action
1. Adequate cash salary.	1. Minimum—$9,200.	1. Review as a committee the Checklist by Lyle Schaller on page 33.	
	1. Desirable—$10,000.	1. Average income in this area is now at $12,000. Source of information was the County Court House.	
	1. To be in line with parish average income and pastoral responsibilities, it would be $12,500.	1. The increase given last year was only equal to the cost of living increase. This cannot be considered a raise.	
		1. This larger figure is $3,000 less than the high-school principal received this year.	
		1. The Lutheran pastor will receive $9,700. The Presbyterian pastor will receive $14,500. The pastor of First United Methodist Church will receive $11,000.	
		1. These proposals were discussed with our judicatory executive and he indicated that he felt that they were in line with salaries for churches the size of ours.	

6
conclusion

For many years I have been an exponent of adequate salaries for pastors whose abilities and productivity are commensurate with the dimension of their calling. In this material I have sought to formalize an approach, from the vantage point of a pastor, to this matter of determining pastoral support. Some pastors will find negotiating a free and natural way to become involved in the process which determines pastoral support, while other pastors may need careful guidance and training before they can be able negotiators. The ability to negotiate in no way reflects on a person's ability to fulfill the role of today's pastor.

Some may suspect that this work was written with only the pastor in mind. This is not the case. My own experience as a pastor for 24 years keeps reminding me that nearly every year, when the subject of pastoral support was before the pastor-parish relations committee, I was asked, "Pastor, what do you think the salary should be?" Many of those 24 years I placed myself and my family's economic life completely in the hands of men and women *who wanted help from me*, but did not get it. Many of their judgments were in my favor, some were not, but few judgments were made on an informed rather than on an emotional base.

I am by training, experience and service a United Methodist. In the United Methodist tradition a key person in creating an atmosphere for negotiating is the district superintendent. District superintendents meet regularly with pastor-parish relations committees (usually annually) and concern themselves with such things as pastoral efficiency, pastoral appointments and pastoral support. If the district superintendent would be familiar with the guidelines in this book, he could give credence to the whole idea of negotiating and establish a style comfortable to both the pastor-parish relations committee and the pastor. The district superintendent might offer data to the pastor-parish relations committee which could be helpful to them as they consider their responsibility to recommend pastoral support. The district superintendent could serve in a dual role, of being helpful to the pastor-parish relations committee as they consult with him, and with the pastor as he develops his proposals.

Since most pastors have no formal training in negotiating, the district superintendent might offer a seminar where pastors could learn and test their skills in negotiating. At that seminar the district superintendent might also help the pastors in his district in the development of their pastor's document.

As was mentioned earlier in Chapter 3, someone outside the parish may serve as a mediator when pastors and committees need outside help. Pastors of the United Methodist tradition have this counsel available in their district superintendent and they should feel free to test their proposals with him.

Other denominations have their moderators, presidents, superintendents, etc. who can serve as consultants and mediators to their pastors in much the same way as district superintendents serve with United Methodist pastors.

The guidelines for negotiating are very simple, and the strategy is in line with the best negotiating processes of today. The style is one of openness and honesty on both sides. For those willing to test and apply these guidelines, this strategy and this process there is real hope for economic respectability for the clergy.

> Some men die by bullets
> Some go down in flames
> But most men perish inch by inch
> While playing little games.
>
> —*Author unknown*

Negotiating is not a little game. It is an honest effort on the part of the pastor to become meaningfully involved in the process which determines pastoral support.

How can the minister do less?

resources for the Pastor

Banker, John C., *Personal Finances for Ministers* (Philadelphia, Pa.: Westminster Press, 1968).

Crawford, John R., *A Christian and His Money* (Nashville, Tenn.: Abingdon Press, 1967).

Glasse, James D., *Profession: Minister* (Nashville, Tenn.: Abingdon Press, 1968).

Gray, Gary M., *The Prophet's Dollar* (New York: Exposition Press, 1971).

Holck, Manfred, *Money Management for Ministers* (Minneapolis, Minn.: Augsburg Publishing House, 1966).

Johnson, Douglas W. and George W. Cornell, *Punctured Preconceptions* (New York: Friendship Press, 1972).

Knight, James A., *For the Love of Money* (Philadelphia, Pa.: J. B. Lippincott Co., 1967).

Packard, Vance, *The Hidden Persuaders* (New York: Pocket Books, 1957).

————*The Waste Makers* (New York: Pocket Books, 1960).

Pocket Data Book (Washington, D. C.: U.S. Department of Commerce, 1971).

Smith, Carlton, Richard Putman Pratt, and the Editors of Time-Life Books, *The Time-Life Books of Family Finance* (New York: Time-Life Books, 1969).

Thal, Helen M., *Your Family and Its Money* (Boston, Mass.: Houghton Mifflin Co., 1968).

The Household Finance Corporation, 919 North Michigan Avenue, Chicago, Ill.

      Money Management Booklets:
         Your Budget
         Children's Spending
         Your Health Dollar
         Your Food Dollar

Your Clothing Dollar
The Shelter Dollar
Home Furnishings
The Recreation Dollar
Your Shopping Dollar
Time Management for Homemakers

A regular reading of *Changing Times* and *Consumers Digest* will provide supportive data.

Community resources:

- Daily newspapers
- Local Labor Unions and U.S. Department of Labor, Bureau of Labor Statistics, Washington, D.C.
- Local Chamber of Commerce
- County Court House
- Pastors of neighboring churches
- Bishops, District Superintendents, Moderators, Synod Presidents, any and all local church administrators.
- Chairperson of pastor-parish relations committees in neighboring churches